Free at Last!

STORIES AND SONGS OF EMANCIPATION

Doreen Rappaport

illustrated by Shane W. Evans

CANDLEWICK PRESS
CAMBRIDGE, MASSACHUSETTS

About This Book

Free at Last! Stories and Songs of Emancipation is the second of three books that I am writing about the experience of black Americans in the United States. This book covers the years from Emancipation in 1863 to the 1954 Supreme Court decision declaring school segregation illegal.

Black abolitionist Frederick Douglass hoped that the end of the Civil War marked the beginning of equality for black Americans. In his newspaper, *The New National Era,* he intended to detail black progress. But the equality that black Americans hoped for quickly vanished with a series of "legal" injustices and violence that made life for Southern blacks more fragile than it had been under slavery. The daily humiliations and continuous brutality against black men, women, and children during this time make it one of the most shameful periods in American history.

Nevertheless, the black community found strength and determination to sustain itself and to fight back. This book traces their courageous struggle to re-create family life and economic independence in the face of overwhelming danger and uncertainty.

As with *No More! Stories and Songs of Slave Resistance*, I searched for voices to tell the story in the most immediate way possible. I found songs, poems, memoirs, letters, and court testimony, and interwove these voices with my own. I followed the thread of slave spirituals, work songs, anthems, and blues. Again, I saw the special place of music and song in articulating feelings and in fortifying and unifying people. I found the poem "Listen Children" by the contemporary poet Lucille Clifton — an inspiring expression of the endurance and self-respect that black Americans passed on to their children.

The dialogue and descriptions of the actions and feelings of Booker T. Washington, Harriet Postle, Jane Kemper, John Solomon Lewis, Ida B. Wells, Kenneth Clark, Jackie Robinson, and Thurgood Marshall come directly from their first-person accounts.

As with *No More! Stories and Songs of Slave Resistance*, I feel fortunate to have artist Shane W. Evans as my collaborator.

I remain in awe of the courage and dignity of Southern blacks and of their inventive defiance and resistance. ◗

Doreen Rappaport

listen children

listen children
keep this in the place
you have for keeping
always
keep it all ways

we have never hated black

listen
we have been ashamed
hopeless   tired   mad
but always
all ways
we loved us

we have always loved each other
children   all ways

pass it on

Lucille Clifton

The Civil War began on April 12, 1861, when Confederate soldiers fired on a federal fort in South Carolina. Eight months later, on January 1, 1863, President Abraham Lincoln issued the Emancipation Proclamation, freeing slaves in the states or parts of states in rebellion. The telegraph brought the news to Boston's Tremont Temple, where abolitionist Frederick Douglass was among the many who rejoiced as a hundred-voice choir sang God's praises. In Washington, D.C., over the roar of cannons fired in celebration, whites and blacks joined in song. As the news traveled through the South, thousands of slaves ran away to join the Union Army.

We were all like the children of Israel in Egypt,
a cryin' and cryin' and a groanin' and groanin',
and no Moses came with the Lord's word
to order the door broke down,
that we might walk through and be free.
Now the big ugly door is broken down,
bless the Lord . . .

ANONYMOUS
circa 1864

6

The Emancipation Proclamation did not at first apply to slave states that remained loyal to the Union. When Maryland's slaves were freed ten months later, owners kidnapped or forcibly took children, as young as five, from their parents. Sympathetic judges enforced "apprenticeship" laws, binding children over as indentured servants. Some parents took matters into their own hands.

The Story of Jane Kemper

Jane Kemper smiles at the sliver of the moon. Maybe luck is with her on this dark night. Step by step, on tiptoe, she inches her way around William Townsend's house. Her former master has stolen her four children. The man at the Freedmen's Bureau said he would try to help her, but he wasn't sure when, so she has come by herself to get them.

She stops at the door leading to the cellar. Did he hide them there? Or in the barn? No, too obvious. Her eyes come to rest on the root cellar across the path, where potatoes are stored for the winter. No, he wouldn't put them there. It's too small for four children. And there can't be enough air to breathe. But . . . he's just cruel enough to do it.

She crawls across the grass and unhooks the root cellar door. She leans her head in and whispers their names, hoping they are still conscious. One by one, they crawl out to join their mother. ▬

The U.S. Supreme Court did not strike down the apprenticeship laws until 1867. Some historians believe as many as ten thousand children were stolen from their parents.

The Civil War ended on April 9, 1865. But not until Congress passed the Thirteenth Amendment, on December 18, 1865, was slavery finally abolished in all the states and territories.

The Story of Booker T. Washington

Nine-year-old Booker T. Washington stands on the porch of his owner's house near Hale's Ford, Virginia. He snuggles into the crook of his mother's arm. A white man in a blue uniform starts to talk. Booker does not understand all his big fancy words, but he senses their importance. When the man finishes speaking, Booker's mother hugs him so tight he can hardly breathe. Tears stream down her face as she kisses Booker and his sister and brother. "I prayed many times for this day," she says, "but I never believed I would live to see it." Then he knows. They are free! Every last one of the slaves on James Burroughs's plantation. The hugging gives way to cries of joy and shouting.

But when Booker's family returns to their cabin, their joyous exuberance has turned to fear. Where will they go? What will they do? Can they make it on their own? They know nothing but the life of the plantation. –

Free at Last

Free at last, free at last, I thank God I'm free at last; Free at last,

1. **2.** *Fine*

free at last,___ I thank God I'm free at last. O free at last.

"Way down yon-der in the grave - yard walk, I thank God I'm
On a my knees when the light pass'd by, I thank God I'm
Some of these morn - ings, bright and fair, I thank God I'm

free at last, Me and my Je - sus goin' to
free at last, Thought my soul would
free at last, Goin' meet King Je - sus

D.C.

meet and talk,_____ I thank God I'm free at last, O
rise and fly, _____ I thank God I'm free at last, O
in the air, _____ I thank God I'm free at last, O

As soon as they were freed, thousands legalized their love in formal marriage ceremonies. Thousands of others set out to find the husbands, wives, and children from whom they had been separated, sometimes for years, when their masters sold them off to new owners. Men and women placed ads in newspapers. They wrote to federal officials, asking for help in finding their families. Most did not succeed. Reunions were often painful and disappointing. Like other black women, Laura Spicer discovered that her husband had a new family:

> *Every time I gits a letter from you it tears me all to pieces. I love you just as well as I did the last day I saw you. And it will not do for you and I to meet. I am married, and my wife have two children. If you and I meets, it would make a very dissatisfied family.*
>
> *Send me some of the children's hair in a separate paper with their names on the paper. It never was our wishes to be separated from each other, and it never was our fault. I had rather anything had happened to me most than ever to have been parted from you.*

The four million newly freed had no money or jobs or homes. Many wandered about looking for shelter and food. Congress set up the Freedmen's Bureau to help reconstruct economic life in the South. The South was divided into five districts, supervised by the Army. Food and medicine were given free to those in need. Army personnel helped the newly freed negotiate work contracts. More than 4,300 free schools were set up and staffed by ex slaves, free blacks, and white Northerners. The education forbidden during slavery was now a reality. Eager eighty-year-olds sat next to five-year-olds and they learned their ABCs together.

White Southerners were determined to prevent their former slaves from ever achieving equality. They drew up Black Codes, severely restricting their rights. Black Americans were forced off the streets after sunset by curfews. They were arrested for trivial offenses and forbidden to testify in court or serve on juries. They could not own guns or hold large meetings.

Liberal Republicans in Congress passed "civil rights" laws, hoping to protect the newly freed. To get back into the Union, Southern states now had to ratify the Fourteenth Amendment, granting citizenship to all people born or naturalized in the U.S. The amendment also stated that state governments could not deprive a person of "life, liberty, or property without due process of law." Tennessee was the only Confederate state to ratify the amendment in the first two years after its proposal.

In May 1866, antiblack riots broke out in Memphis. Three months later, white mobs attacked an integrated group meeting to discuss black suffrage. On night rides, secret vigilante groups terrorized black men, women, and children.

The Story of Harriet Postle

Harriet Postle shifts her weight from side to side in bed. It is hard finding a comfortable sleeping position when you are seven months pregnant. She reaches over to touch her husband, when she hears a thundering noise outside.

"Postle, we know you're in there! You'd better come out!"

Harriet knows who is yelling — the Ku Klux Klan men wearing masks, tall pointed caps, and long white robes.

Her oldest son wakes and ducks under the
mattress. The baby wakes and starts to fuss. Her
husband darts out of bed, loosens three floorboards,
and jumps into the hiding place they prepared
months ago. She replaces the planks. She steps into
her skirt to cover her nightshirt, but she is so
flustered she gets entangled in the material.
"Postle! Open up this door! You can't
hide from us!"

Harriet scoops up the baby and plops down in a chair over the hiding place. She puts her hands over the baby's ears, trying to block out the furious banging.

The door crashes in. Four men in dusty boots point pistols at the mattress, under which her son cowers.

"Leave my boy alone!" she shouts.

One man jerks her chair out from under her. She falls to the floor, hugging her baby. The man stomps his foot on her huge stomach. "Where is your husband?"

"He's not here!"

He drops a rope shaped like a noose over her neck. "Tell me where he is." Her son is screaming and sobbing at the same time. The baby wails. The man presses harder on her stomach. "Where is he?"

She does not answer. She will not betray her husband.

It seems like a miracle but the men finally leave. Her husband comes out of hiding. She cradles her children in her arms, but she cannot stop their crying. ▬

On July 28, 1868, the Fourteenth Amendment finally became law. But the vigilantes kept riding.

Black activists campaigned to get the vote for black men. On March 30, 1870, the Fifteenth Amendment, granting suffrage, became law. In five Southern states, blacks soon became the majority of voters. They used the power of the ballot to elect black men at every level of government. Portraits of these new public servants decorated black homes. They were postmasters, state court justices, superintendents of education, legislators, governors, and lieutenant governors. By 1874, more than 1,500 black men had been elected to office in the South.

The night rides increased. Klan members burned elected officials out of their homes. They shot at them, stabbed them, and whipped them. Thirty-four black office-holders were murdered.

Congress passed more laws to protect blacks, but white Southerners kept dreaming up new ways to keep them down. Blacks were given tests: they had to interpret state constitutions to prove "qualified" (intelligent enough) to vote. Poor blacks could not afford the required poll tax. Under the grandfather clause, you could vote only if your father or grandfather was eligible to vote or if you had an ancestor in the Confederate or Union Army. Black lawmakers denounced the grandfather clause, which stripped most black men of the right to vote. They brought legal actions in court, and lost.

Portraits on facing page:

John S. Rock: justice of the peace, Boston, Massachusetts, 1861.

Matthew Gaines: U.S. senator, Texas, 1869–1873.

P. B. S. Pinchback: governor, Louisiana, 1872–1873.

W. Hines Furbush: U.S. congressman, Arkansas, 1873–1874 and 1879–1880.

John Mercer Langston: dean of the Law Department, Howard University, Washington, D.C., 1868–1875; U.S. congressman, Virginia, 1888–1890; next to Frederick Douglass, the most prominent and influential African American of the nineteenth century.

John R. Lynch: U.S. congressman, Mississippi, 1872–1876.

Congress promised every black man forty acres. Some land was distributed until Black Codes forbade blacks from owning land. They had little choice but to rent land from whites. Sharecropping — a new form of slavery — was born. Under this system, owners were *supposed* to split the profits of a harvest with renters, but most black farmers ended up in debt. Faced with few economic opportunities, daily humiliations, and escalating violence, tens of thousands of African Americans fled the South. The largest number, called the Exodusters, went to Kansas.

The Story of John Solomon Lewis

John Solomon Lewis watches the *Grant Tower* pull in to the dock. In the last three weeks, many boats have refused to pick up the black families waiting to go to Kansas. He cannot let that happen again. It is fourteen years since Emancipation, but he does not feel free in Tensas Parish, Louisiana. Three weeks ago he told his landlord that he was leaving. The man threatened to blow his head off. That night, Lewis and his family stole into the forest.

"Where's you going?" the ship's captain asks.

"Kansas," Lewis answers for the group.

"You can't go on this boat," says the captain.

Lewis will not be stopped this time. "Oh yes, I can," he says defiantly. "Do you know who I am? I was a Union soldier. I know my rights. If my family isn't allowed on this boat, I'll take you to court and sue for damages."

The captain is shocked by his defiance.

"Let this nigger on or he'll make trouble," the first mate whispers to the captain.

The captain steps aside, and John Solomon Lewis leads his family and the long line of black men, women, and children onto the *Grant Tower*. ▪

Most Exodusters arrived with little or no money. They could not buy livestock or farming tools or seed. They had nothing to eat. Some arrived barefoot when deep snow covered the earth. Despite these hardships, few returned south.

Southern white legislators passed laws separating whites and blacks on public transportation. In 1881, the four black lawmakers in Tennessee's state legislature pressed for another law forbidding race discrimination on railroads. White lawmakers responded by writing another law allowing "separate but equal" facilities. Some individuals spontaneously challenged segregation.

The Story of Ida B. Wells

Ida B. Wells slips her ticket into her pocket and climbs the steps of the train. She walks briskly toward the first-class coach. All "ladies" sit in first class. She rests her overnight bag on her seat.

"Tickets, please," the conductor chants. When he reaches Wells, he leans over her seat. "You must leave this car," he orders, grabbing her belongings.

She hands him her ticket without looking up. "I'm a lady. All ladies sit here," she answers.

"I will treat you like a lady, but you must go to the other car."

"If you wish to treat me like a lady, leave me alone."

He grabs her wrists. She pushes her feet into the seat in front of her. He pulls harder. She digs her teeth into his hand. She bites so hard, she draws blood.

"Get out of here," the white passengers shout. She does not move. "Get out of here!" They keep screaming until two white men carry her and her seat out of the first-class car. Wells ignores the jeers and cheers as she steps off the train. ▪

Ida B. Wells sued the Chesapeake, Ohio, and South Western Railway Company and won two hundred dollars in damages. When the same thing happened again, she sued a second time and won five hundred dollars. The railroad appealed. The case reached the Tennessee State Supreme Court, where the judges ruled against Wells.

In 1896, a similar case, *Plessy v. Ferguson*, reached the U.S. Supreme Court. Homer Plessy's lawyers argued that segregated trains were illegal because the Fourteenth Amendment guaranteed equal protection for all Americans. The Court ruled that it was *not* illegal if the separate accommodations were equal. The next few years saw scattered group protests in Georgia and Mississippi, but race segregation triumphed.

Blacks and whites did not attend the same schools, sit next to each other on buses or trains, drink from the same water fountains, use the same libraries, or eat in the same restaurants. In truth, "separate but equal" accommodations did not exist. All black facilities were inferior.

Incident

(for Eric Walrond)

Once riding in old Baltimore,
  Heart-filled, head-filled with glee,
I saw a Baltimorean
  Keep looking straight at me.

Now I was eight and very small,
  And he was no whit bigger,
And so I smiled, but he poked out
  His tongue, and called me, "Nigger."

I saw the whole of Baltimore
  From May until December;
Of all the things that happened there
  That's all that I remember.

COUNTEE CULLEN

The campaign to intimidate black Southerners continued. Black men, women, and children were arrested for petty offenses. "Mischief, insulting gestures, cruel treatment to animals, and selling liquor" landed long jail sentences.

Southern governors did not have enough money to build prisons for these "criminals." A new business arose — leasing convicts. Black prisoners were hired out six and seven days a week to do the backbreaking jobs that free Americans did not want to do. Southern businesses finally had cheap labor again, and millions of dollars poured into the state coffers. Convict leasing, like sharecropping, was slavery under a new name.

They picked cotton in Mississippi,
boiled and cured sugar in Texas,
coaxed sap from pine trees in Florida,
pulled up roots in swamps in Alabama,
loaded and unloaded bricks in Georgia,
and chipped away at coal in Tennessee.
If they stopped for even a minute,
the whipping boss brought out
    "Old Suzie."

At night, shackled together,
they lay on blood-stained dirt floors
or on grime-covered wooden slabs,
in tents
or in dark, airless huts
or in iron cages without screens.
Flies buzzed around their heads.
Fleas nipped at their bodies.

Rats ran over their legs.
They breathed the stench of sweat
and the night bucket
and plotted their escape
before falling off to sleep.

When the investigators finally came
and asked, "How are you?"
they answered, "Fine. Just fine."
They knew if they didn't, at night
the whipping boss would bring out
    "Old Suzie"
and lash their backs and arms
until they were senseless
or taken to be buried in "nigger hill."
It did not matter if a convict died,
for if one died, they got another.

Doreen Rappaport

Despite shackles, whippings,
and guards with rifles,
convict escapes were
a constant problem.

27

Added to the threat of imprisonment was the fear of being lynched. Between 1889 and 1918, there were 3,224 lynchings. Seventy-eight percent of the victims were black.

In 1892, three well-respected black men were lynched in Memphis, Tennessee. Their murders horrified reporter Ida B. Wells. She investigated the reasons for many lynchings and found proof that "uppity" blacks were often accused of murder or rape, and executed before having a trial. In a blazing editorial in her newspaper, the *Memphis Free Speech*, she wrote:

> *Southern whites should tell the truth and admit that colored men and women are lynched for almost any offense, from murder to a misdemeanor. Nobody believes the old threadbare lie that Negro men rape white women. Southern white men justify their own barbarism by assuming a chivalry they do not possess. True chivalry respects all womanhood.*

Angry whites ransacked her office and threatened her with death. She fled Memphis but continued her antilynching campaign for the rest of her life.

Lynchings were often public spectacles. White Southerners traveled hundreds of miles to witness innocent people being hung, shot, or dismembered. Women nursed their babies while watching whippings and brandings. Parents hoisted their children up on their shoulders to give them a clear view of a man being roasted to death. Sometimes after the hanging, just for fun, the mob pumped the victim with bullets.

In a world of violence and humiliation, African Americans worked hard to instill pride in their children. Benjamin Mays's mother was not the only black mother who told her child, "You are as good as anybody." Children learned that it was their parents' and grandparents' labor in the rice, cotton, and tobacco fields that had made the South rich. They were taught the proud history of Underground Railroad conductor Harriet Tubman, and of abolitionists Frederick Douglass and Sojourner Truth.

There was strength and comfort from church and community. On Sundays, people sang and prayed, surrounded by friends and relatives. Forbidden in city parks, black children played baseball at church picnics. Some communities built their own schools to educate their young. Black women formed associations and raised money for orphanages, homes for the aged, and settlement houses. The motto of the National Association of Colored Women was "Lifting as We Climb."

As during slavery, music remained a powerful weapon to sustain the spirit. Children felt great pride when singing about the legendary railroad worker, John Henry. He was so strong that he was pitted in a contest against a machine to see who could dig through the mountain faster. John Henry symbolizes the strength and resilience of all African Americans who helped build the nation.

John Henry

1873

John __ Hen - ry said __ to his cap - tain, "A __ man ain't noth-in' but a man, 'Fore I'll let this steam drill beat me down, I'll die with my ham - mer in my hand, Lord, Die with my ham - mer in my hand."

That man that hold that steam drill
Thought he was mighty fine,
John Henry hammered steel, drove ten feet,
While the steam drill only made it nine, Lord,
While the steam drill only made it nine.

In June 1881, when teacher Booker T. Washington arrived in Tuskegee, Alabama, he found that there was no school building. The African Methodist Episcopal Church lent him a dilapidated shack while he looked for a proper building. A former teacher of his lent him money to buy a hundred-acre farm.

His students cleaned and painted the stable, built desks and chairs. They raked the rocky soil and grew vegetables. They dug clay for bricks and built a proper school. Poor blacks in the county shared their hard-earned pennies and nickels and dimes and eggs and milk and pigs.

Washington needed money for equipment to teach carpentry, blacksmithing, shoemaking, and tinsmithing. He went north. Wealthy white Northerners liked when Washington said that blacks had to "uplift" themselves from their "lowly position" as slaves. They admired his self-reliant students. They gave him money. Tuskegee Institute grew, and so did Washington's reputation as an educator, even among white Southerners.

The Story of Booker T. Washington

An audience of two thousand applauds when Georgia's former governor announces that "a great Southern educator" will now speak. But when the white people in the audience see Booker T. Washington walk to the dais, their hands freeze. How can a Negro be a great educator?

In a quiet, dignified voice, Washington says: "To my race I say, cast down your bucket where you are. The masses of us are to live by our hands. No race can prosper until it learns that there is as much dignity in tilling a field as in writing a poem. It is at the bottom of life we must begin and not the top. . . .

"To those of the white race, I say, cast down your bucket among the eight million Negroes. We are the most patient, faithful, law abiding, and unresentful people the world has ever seen. We have proved our loyalty in the past, nursing your children and your mothers and fathers. In the future, we shall lay down our lives, if need be, in defense of yours."

He raises his hand and spreads his fingers. "In all things that are purely social, we can be as separate as the fingers, yet one as the hand in all things essential to mutual progress."

White men cheer and toss their hats. White women wave their handkerchiefs. Booker T. is *their* kind of Negro. He knows his place. ▪

Washington's speech of September 18, 1895, was reprinted and praised in newspapers all over the country. White Americans considered Washington the leading black spokesperson until his death in 1915.

Washington's "policy of accommodation" did nothing to stop white violence. It remained a challenge every day to stay alive. As during slavery, black Southerners hid their feelings as a form of survival and resistance.

We Wear the Mask

We wear the mask that grins and lies,
  It hides our cheeks and shades our eyes,—
This debt we pay to human guile;
With torn and bleeding hearts we smile,
And mouth with myriad subtleties.

Why should the world be over-wise,
In counting all our tears and sighs?
Nay, let them only see us, while
  We wear the mask.

We smile, but, O great Christ, our cries
To Thee from tortured souls arise.
We sing, but oh the clay is vile
Beneath our feet, and long the mile;
But let the world dream otherwise,
  We wear the mask!

PAUL LAURENCE DUNBAR

37

Educator John Hope and publisher Monroe Trotter denounced Booker T. Washington's ideas at public meetings. Ida B. Wells attacked him in print for statements that appeared to excuse lynchings. In *The Souls of Black Folk*, scholar W. E. B. Du Bois explained why Washington was "leading the way backward":

> *The problem of the twentieth century is the problem of the color-line — the relation of the darker to the lighter races of men. Mr. Washington represents in Negro thought the old attitude of adjustment and submission. His program practically accepts the alleged inferiority of the Negro races. On the whole, his doctrine has tended to make whites, North and South, shift the burden of the Negro problem to the Negro's shoulders, when in fact the burden belongs to the nation.*

Du Bois and Trotter spearheaded the Niagara Movement, which demanded the same rights as white Americans. In February 1909, its members joined with other black and white activists to form the National Association for the Advancement of Colored People (NAACP). Du Bois became director of publicity and research, and editor of its newsletter, *The Crisis*. NAACP lawyers began challenging segregation laws. Their first important victory came in 1915 when the U.S. Supreme Court declared the grandfather clauses unconstitutional.

In 1900, James Weldon Johnson and his brother, J. Rosamond Johnson, wrote a song for a schoolchildren's celebration of Abraham Lincoln's birthday in Jacksonville, Florida. Over time, those children became teachers and parents and taught the song to other children. "Lift Ev'ry Voice and Sing" gradually became known as the Negro National Anthem. In 1920, it became the official song of the NAACP. It is still one of the most cherished songs of African Americans.

Lift Ev'ry Voice and Sing

Moderato e maestoso

Lift ev - 'ry voice and sing, Till earth and hea - ven
Ston - y the road we trod, Bit - ter the chast - 'ning

ring, Ring with the har - mo - nies of Lib - er -
rod, Felt in the days when hope un - born had

ty; Let our re - joic - ing rise High as the list - 'ning
died; Yet with a stead - y beat, Have not our wear - y

skies, Let it re - sound loud as the roll - ing sea.
feet Come to the place for which our fa - thers sighed?

Sing a song full of the faith that the dark past has taught us.
We have come ov - er a way that with tears has been wa - tered.

rall. e molto cresc.　　　　　　　　　　　　allargando

Sing a song full of the hope that the pres - ent has brought
We have come, tread - ing our path thro' the blood of the slaugh -

ff a tempo

us; Fac - ing the ris - ing sun Of our new day be -
tered, Out from the gloom - y past, Till now we stand at

gun, Let us march on till vic - to - ry is won.
last Where the white gleam of our bright star is cast.

In the 1890s, the boll weevil devastated cotton crops in the Deep South and as far west as Texas. Tens of thousands of black sharecroppers went north, where there were jobs. The year 1913 saw floods in Mississippi. War broke out in Europe the following year. Northern factories needed more workers to fulfill wartime contracts. They sent agents south to recruit blacks. Over a million Southern blacks migrated north to Chicago, Detroit, Pittsburgh, Cleveland, and New York City. Their trickster tales and stories of slave resistance traveled with them. So did their unique music — spirituals, ragtime, work songs, hollers, jazz, and blues.

Jazz trumpeter Sidney Bechet described a black prisoner singing the blues: "He was more than just a man. He was like every man that's been done a wrong. Inside him he'd got the memory of all the wrong that's been done to all my people. When I remember that man, I'm remembering myself, a feeling I've always had."

If you don't believe I'm sinking
Just look at the hole I'm in
If you don't believe I'm bound up in trouble
Just look at the color of my skin.

ANONYMOUS

In the 1920s, black artists and intellectuals gravitated to Harlem, a neighborhood in upper Manhattan. It was a time of racial consciousness and artistic expression. Black nationalist Marcus Garvey preached self-respect, and thousands marched in his parades. Arthur Schomburg tracked down documents and artifacts proving Africa's rich history. Carter G. Woodson wrote *The Negro in Our History.* Katherine Dunham created dances based on her travels to Africa and the Caribbean. Jacob Lawrence painted the mass migrations of blacks to Northern cities. Augusta Savage created a sculpture based on "Lift Ev'ry Voice and Sing." Zora Neale Hurston wrote about rural life. James P. Johnson and Fats Waller played a new blend of ragtime and jazz called piano stride. And "Shuffle Along," the first musical written and performed by blacks, opened on Broadway.

Poet Langston Hughes adored Harlem's energy and beauty, but like all artists of the Harlem Renaissance, he could not ignore the racism that also existed in the North. The "Promised Land" had segregated housing and schools. White labor unions didn't want blacks competing for jobs. Black men who had fought valiantly in the "War for Democracy" in Europe came home and found the same racism as before. There was segregation even in Harlem: only whites or blacks light enough to pass for white were admitted to the Cotton Club, the prestigious Harlem nightclub.

Despite the continuing hardships and humiliations and violence, Hughes celebrated the enduring strength of his people.

I, Too, Sing America

I am the darker brother.
They send me to eat in the kitchen
When company comes,
But I laugh,
And eat well,
And grow strong.

Tomorrow,
I'll be at the table
When company comes.
Nobody'll dare
Say to me,
"Eat in the kitchen,"
Then.

Besides,
They'll see how beautiful I am
And be ashamed—

I, too, am America.

LANGSTON HUGHES

In 1929, the stock market crashed and millions of Americans were out of work. In 1933, when Franklin Delano Roosevelt became president, the federal government created jobs. Americans built hospitals, schools, community centers, and playgrounds. Black leaders protested because too few African Americans were hired for these jobs. After Germany invaded Poland in 1939, hundreds of thousands of white men were hired to build weapons for our allies. Black leaders insisted that some of these jobs go to their people. Nothing was done.

A. Philip Randolph, head of the union called the Brotherhood of Sleeping Car Porters, planned a protest march on Washington. President Roosevelt tried to convince him to call it off. Randolph refused. Six days before the march, Roosevelt issued an executive order barring discrimination in hiring in defense industries and government agencies. Randolph called off the march, but continued his campaign to desegregate the armed forces.

Under pressure from black leaders, in October 1941, the U.S. Air Force began training black men to be pilots. Despite their excellent skills, prejudice kept the Ninety-ninth Fighter Squadron, or Tuskegee Airmen, from combat overseas. On April 15, 1943, they were finally sent to North Africa. Again disappointment and anger, for they were shut out of combat and assigned only to support operations. General Benjamin O. Davis Jr. fought to get his pilots assigned to bombing missions. Finally, in October 1943, they began flying in formation with white pilots. Their courage and skill earned them hundreds of awards.

But A. Philip Randolph was not satisfied, for the other branches of service were still segregated. In 1948, Randolph organized pickets at the Democratic National Convention. Wanting African Americans to vote for him, President Harry S. Truman issued an executive order ending segregation in the armed forces.

In 1947, *major league baseball was segregated.* Brooklyn Dodgers manager Branch Rickey hired Jackie Robinson to "break the color line." Rickey knew how difficult this would be. He made Robinson promise that for three years he would not fight back or answer back no matter how tough things got.

The Story of Jackie Robinson

"Hey, nigger why don't you go back to the cotton field where you belong?"

"They're waiting for you in the jungles, black boy!"

Jackie Robinson steps up to the plate in the first inning. He taps his cleats with his bat and pretends not to hear the abuse coming from the fans and from the dugout of the Philadelphia Phillies. Their manager, a Southerner, is fuming at Rickey for hiring a Negro.

"We don't want you here, nigger!"

Robinson readies his stance for the pitch, but the ball flies by before he can swing.

"Strike one!"

"Go back to the bushes!"

What am I doing here turning the other cheek as though I'm not a man? In my whole life I never let anyone talk to me this way. To hell with Mr. Rickey's noble experiment. It's not going to succeed.

The pitcher winds up and fires a second ball.

"Go back to the jungle!"

Robinson pops up a foul for strike two.

"Knew you couldn't do it, nigger!"

"That's enough from you, boy!"

How wonderful it would be to throw down my bat, walk over to the Phillies' dugout, grab one of them, and smash his teeth in with my despised black fist. I could walk away from it all right now.

Robinson breathes deeply. *No, I won't.* He looks up at the ball zooming toward him. Again, he's too late to swing.

"Strike three!"

By the bottom of the eighth inning, the game is still tied at 0–0. Then Robinson gets a single. Crouched down on first, he watches the pitcher throw to the next batter. Now! Robinson steals second. The catcher throws the ball to second, but Robinson is already on his way to third. When the next Dodger whacks the ball, Robinson runs home, breaking the tie. ▬

The jeering never stopped that first year, but Jackie Robinson played great ball anyway. He finished the season batting .297. He led the Dodgers in home runs and led the league in stolen bases. He was named National League Rookie of the Year. He played all ten years of his major league career with the Dodgers and remains one of baseball's greatest and most beloved players.

By 1949, the NAACP had won enough cases to begin chipping away at race segregation laws. But lawyer Thurgood Marshall knew that the U.S. Supreme Court justices had to be convinced to overturn the "separate but equal" decision in the 1896 *Plessy v. Ferguson* case. He had to prove to them that segregation violated the Fourteenth Amendment. He had to show them that separate schools damaged black children. He asked psychologist Kenneth Clark to help.

The Story of Kenneth Clark

Lawyers Robert Carter and Thurgood Marshall sit in the back of a classroom in Clarendon County, South Carolina. Across the room, Dr. Kenneth Clark sits at a table with a seven-year-old black girl. Two black men stand at the door to protect the three Northerners. If white people in town learn why they are here, there could be trouble.

Clark puts a black doll and a white doll on the table. "Which doll do you like better?" he asks the seven-year-old.

She points to the white doll. "The black doll looks bad," she adds.

"Which doll is black?" he asks. She points to the doll with the black face.

"Which doll is white?" She points to the doll with the pink face.

"Show me the doll that's most like you."

The little girl does not answer the question.

"Which doll is most like you?" he asks again.

She quickly points to the black doll, then looks away as if wanting to forget what she said. ▬

Clark asked sixteen black children, ages six to nine, the same questions. Ten children said they liked the white doll better than the black doll. Eleven added that the black doll looked "bad." Many children became upset when asked to identify the doll most like them. Seven children said they saw themselves as the white doll.

Thurgood Marshall had his proof that segregation made black children believe that they were inferior to whites. He would use this evidence in his legal case that school segregation was illegal.

In December 1952, five cases involving school segregation reached the U.S. Supreme Court. *Brown v. Board of Education of Topeka, Kansas,* was one case: Denied admission to her local school because of race, seven-year-old Linda Brown had to cross railroad tracks and wait for a bus to drive her to a segregated school.

The Story of Thurgood Marshall

Thurgood Marshall walks past hundreds of unfamiliar faces outside the Supreme Court building. These people have stood here for hours, hoping to hear him argue this case. Marshall is scared to death about what the justices will decide.

He listens carefully as the justices ask question after question. Often they interrupt him before he finishes answering. He waits for the right moment to counter something said the day before:

"I got the feeling on hearing the discussion yesterday that when you put a white child in the school with colored children, the white child would fall apart. Everybody knows that this is not true. These same kids in Virginia and South Carolina play in the street together. They play on their farms together. They go down the road together. They separate to go to school. They come out of school and play ball together. Why do you single out Negroes for this separate treatment? The only reason can be a determination that people formerly in slavery shall be kept as near that stage as possible. Now is the time that this court must make it clear that this is not what the Constitution stands for." ▬

Eighteen months later, on Monday, May 17, 1954, Chief Justice Earl Warren announced the court's unanimous opinion: the doctrine of "separate but equal" was unconstitutional. Separate educational facilities were inherently unequal.

Marshall had done what his law professor Charles Houston had taught him. He had challenged the white man's law and won this landmark decision before an all-white court.

Ain't I Glad I've Got Out the Wilderness

O, ain't I glad I've got out the wil-der-ness, Got out the wil-der-ness,

got out the wil-der-ness, Ain't I glad I've got out the wil-der-ness,

Lean-ing on the Lord, O, ain't I glad I've Lord.

Refrain

Come a-lean-ing on the Lord, Come a-lean-ing on the Lord, Come a-

lean-ing on the Lamb of God that takes a-way the sins of the world.

Marshall knew the struggle
was not over. The Court had not
stated how and when school
segregation was to end.
And what about segregation
on public transportation and in
restaurants and in hospitals?

There would be
more battles ahead
until integration was
the way of the country.

Important Dates

January 1, 1863. The Emancipation Proclamation ends slavery in the territory in rebellion.

March 3, 1865. The U.S. Congress establishes the Bureau of Refugees, Freedmen, and Abandoned Lands, usually called the Freedmen's Bureau, to help the newly freed slaves adjust to freedom.

April 9, 1865. Confederate General Robert E. Lee surrenders to General Ulysses S. Grant.

December 18, 1865. The Thirteenth Amendment to the Constitution outlaws slavery and all forms of involuntary servitude.

April 9, 1866. The Civil Rights Act gives blacks the rights of full citizenship—to make contracts, hold property, testify in court—and declares them responsible to the laws, punishments, and penalties of the United States.

July 28, 1868. The Fourteenth Amendment, providing for federal protection of the civil rights of blacks, is ratified. It guarantees the right to vote to African American men.

March 30, 1870. The Fifteenth Amendment secures the vote for black men.

May 31, 1870. Congress passes the first Enforcement Act to help enforce the Fifteenth Amendment.

1870. *New National Era* newspaper is founded in Washington, D.C. Frederick Douglass is its corresponding editor.

March 1, 1875. A Civil Rights Act forbids discrimination in public accommodations. Eight years later the U.S. Supreme Court declares the act unconstitutional.

1877–1899. Former Confederate states pass poll tax laws to restrict voting by black Americans.

1879. Southern blacks emigrate to Kansas, Oklahoma, and California.

September 18, 1895. Booker T. Washington gives his "Atlanta Compromise" speech.

1895. Ida B. Wells publishes *A Red Record*.

May 18, 1896. *Plessy v. Ferguson* justifies segregation by race.

1896. Louisiana passes the first of the grandfather clauses.

February 12, 1909. The National Association for the Advancement of Colored People (NAACP) is founded.

April 6, 1917. The United States enters World War I.

1920s. During the Harlem Renaissance, black artists achieve prominence.

December 12, 1938. In *Missouri ex rel. Gaines v. Canada, Registrar of the University of Missouri, et al.,* the U.S. Supreme Court rules that states have to provide equal educational opportunities for blacks, even if they are separate.

June 25, 1941. President Roosevelt issues Executive Order 8802, barring discrimination in hiring in defense industries and government agencies.

April 10, 1947. Jackie Robinson becomes the first black major league baseball player.

July 26, 1948. President Truman issues Executive Order 9981, ending discrimination in the armed forces.

May 17, 1954. In *Brown v. Board of Education of Topeka, Kansas,* the U.S. Supreme Court rules that racial segregation in public schools is unconstitutional and that separate is inherently unequal.

ARTIST'S NOTE

History, to me, is an odd and amorphous construct that people tend to compartmentalize and call their own, when in fact it is our own. The word *history* itself is suspect. If you break the word down, it can be read as "his story." For the sake of how I feel, let's rename it "ourstory." It's easy to forget that, while individual stories are unfolding, a parallel "ourstory" is evolving. We are all connected, and the joy and pain that visits others will visit us because it is our joy and pain.

Growing up in a racially mixed family, I had the unique opportunity to sample the cultures of two distinct groups. Society may try to categorize me as African American because of my skin tone, but do I ignore who I truly am because others can't see it? Through Doreen Rappaport's efforts and words I have learned about the person I am, but more important, I have learned about the people we all are. In the case of the author-illustrator union, when one person appears European American (white) and one person appears African American (black), what we have forged is truly a telling of "ourstory."

Using the medium of expression that I love to bring to life the struggles of our people is a blessing in itself. Some of the struggles and conflicts cited in this book could not even have been visualized and expressed by the people who lived them not so long ago. I don't have to reach that far back in "mystory" to touch those—my mother, my father, my family—who fought for me and the opportunities I have, and I am grateful.

In this "politically correct" world, it is easy to lose sight of the fact that we continue to be divided by boundaries of our own making. We continually fail to realize that we are all simply human. So as you read the words and gaze at the images in this "ourstory," put yourselves in the shoes of these people who fought and loved so hard, for they are all of us.

Many blessings,

Shane W. Evans

Acknowledgments

I thank the superb reference librarians at the Schomburg Center for Black Culture for their help, and Brenna Tinkel and Sharon Harrison for their research skills and insight. I thank Dorothy Carter, Professor Emeritas of Children's Literature, Bank Street College of Education, for critiquing the manuscript.

"Everytime I gits a letter from you . . ." was found in *Dear Ones at Home: Letters from the Contraband Camps.* The name of the man who wrote the letter was not given. "We were all like the children of Israel . . ." was found in Leon F. Litwak's *Been in the Storm So Long: The Aftermath of Slavery.* The original source was a newspaper article in the *New York Tribune,* dated April 6, 1865, which described the sermon of an unnamed black preacher in Nashville, Tennessee. Sidney Bechet's quote and "If you don't believe I'm sinking . . ." (author anonymous) were found in Lawrence W. Levine's *Black Culture and Black Consciousness: Afro-American Folk Thought from Slavery to Freedom.* (Lawrence W. Levine and Leon F. Litwak have synthesized invaluable musical and oral traditional sources that help us understand the uniqueness and richness of black music and story.)

While researching convict leasing, I found a quote from Hasting H. Hart in the report *Prison Conditions in the South,* given before the National Prison Association in 1919. I was horrified by the casualness with which Mr. Hart said that, during slavery, "if a man had a good Negro he could afford to keep him . . . but we don't own 'em. One dies, get another," and so I worked the phrase into my poem on convict leasing.

Thurgood Marshall's testimony was edited from his arguments in *Brown v. Board of Education of Topeka, Kansas.* Harriet Postle's testimony before a Congressional Committee investigating Klan terror in 1872 was used to write her vignette. The quotes by W. E. B. Du Bois, Ida B. Wells, Booker T. Washington, and Laura Spicer's husband were shortened without changing their meaning.

Material by Lucille Clifton, Ida B. Wells, W. E. B. Du Bois, Paul Laurence Dunbar, Langston Hughes, and Booker T. Washington is noted in Selected Sources. Spirituals and work songs were passed orally from generation to generation.

Many of these songs were transcribed by interested performers and folklorists; their versions vary. I kept some words as transcribed because they effectively transmit the rhythm and feelings of the songs, but changed others, choosing words and spellings that would be most accessible to children. I changed the dialect in the sermon on page 6 because it resembled too many black speeches transcribed and caricatured by whites during that era.

The statistics for the number of antiblack riots are horrifying, and new scholarship is continuously updating those numbers. The following dates and places from the turn of the century to the mid-1920s comprise a list of riots involving large numbers of people but should in no way be considered a complete list. These dates and places reveal that African Americans were always in danger no matter where they lived, North or South.

1898: Phoenix, South Carolina;
      Wilmington, North Carolina
1899: Pana, Illinois
1900: Palmetto, Georgia; New Orleans, Louisiana;
      New York, New York
1905: Brownsville, Texas; Atlanta, Georgia;
      New York, New York
1908: Houston, Texas; Springfield, Illinois
1917: East St. Louis, Missouri; Houston, Texas
1919: riots in twenty-five cities
1921: Tulsa, Oklahoma
1924: Niles, Ohio

PERMISSIONS

Hughes, Langston. "I, Too, Sing America." From *The Collected Poems of Langston Hughes*, copyright © 1994 by The Estate of Langston Hughes. Used by permission of Alfred A. Knopf, a division of Random House, Inc.

"Listen Children" copyright 1972 by Lucille Clifton. First appeared in *Good News About the Earth*, published by Random House. Reprinted by permission of Curtis Brown, Ltd.

SELECTED SOURCES

Clifton, Lucille. *Good News About the Earth*. New York: Random House, 1972.

Cullen, Countee. *On These I Stand*. New York: Harper and Brothers, 1925.

Du Bois, W. E. B. *The Souls of Black Folk: essays and sketches*. Chicago: A. C. McClurg & Co.; Cambridge, Mass.: University Press, John Wilson and Son, 1903.

Dunbar, Paul Laurence. *Lyrics of a Lowly Life*. New York: Dodd, Mead, 1896.

Gutman, Herbert George. *The Black Family in Slavery and Freedom, 1750-1925*. New York: Pantheon, 1976.

Levine, Lawrence W. *Black Culture and Black Consciousness: Afro-American Folk Thought from Slavery to Freedom*. New York: Oxford University Press, 1977.

Litwak, Leon F. *Been in the Storm So Long: The Aftermath of Slavery*. New York: Knopf, 1979.

———. *Trouble in Mind: Black Southerners in the Age of Jim Crow*. New York: Knopf, 1998.

Mancini, Matthew J. *One Dies, Get Another: Convict Leasing in the American South, 1866-1928*. Columbia, S.C.: University of South Carolina Press, 1996.

McMurry, Linda O. *To Keep the Waters Troubled: The Life of Ida B. Wells*. New York: Oxford University Press, 1998.

Oshinsky, David M. *"Worse Than Slavery": Parchmen Farm and the Order of Jim Crow Justice*. New York: Free Press, 1996.

Painter, Nell Irvin. *Exodusters: Black Migration to Kansas after Reconstruction*. New York: Knopf, 1977.

Robinson, Jackie. *Jackie Robinson: My Own Story*, as told by Jackie Robinson to Wendell Smith. New York: Greenberg, 1948.

Sterling, Dorothy. *The Trouble They Seen: Black People Tell the Story of Reconstruction*. Garden City, N.Y.: Doubleday, 1976.

———. *We Are Your Sisters: Black Women in the Nineteenth Century*. New York: W. W. Norton, 1984.

Swint, Henry L., ed. *Dear Ones at Home: Letters from Contraband Camps*. Nashville: Vanderbilt University Press, 1966.

Tygiel, Jules. *Baseball's Great Experiment: Jackie Robinson and His Legacy*. New York: Oxford University Press, 1997.

Washington, Booker T. "On the Solution of the Negro Problem." Address delivered at the opening of the Atlanta Cotton States and Exposition, September 18, 1895. Reprinted in *The Negro and the Atlanta Exposition*, by Alice M. Bacon. Baltimore, 1896. The Trustees of the John F. Slater Fund Occasional Papers, No. 7.

Washington, Booker T. *Up from Slavery*. Garden City, N.Y.: Doubleday, 1963.

Wells, Ida. Editorial. *The Memphis Free Speech*. May 21, 1892.

Wells-Barnett, Ida B. *On Lynchings: Southern Horrors, a Red Record, Mob Rule in New Orleans*. New York: Arnold Press, 1969, reprint.

To learn more about the people and events in this book, you can read:

Arthur, Joe. *Justice for All: The Story of Thurgood Marshall*. New York: Bantam Doubleday Dell Book for Young Readers, 1994.

Clifton, Lucille. *Blessing the Boats: New and Selected Poems, 1988-2000*. Rochester, N.Y.: BOA Editions, 2000.

Cooper, Floyd. *Coming Home: From the Life of Langston Hughes*. New York: Philomel Books, 1994.

Denenberg, Barry. *Stealing Home: The Story of Jackie Robinson*. New York: Scholastic, 1997.

Freedman, Suzanne. *Ida B. Wells-Barnett and the Antilynching Crusade*. Brookfield, Conn.: Millbrook Press, 1994.

Haskins, Jim. *Black Eagles: African Americans in Aviation*. New York: Scholastic, 1996.

Lawler, Mary. *Marcus Garvey: Black Nationalist Leader*. Broomall, Penn.: Chelsea House, 1988.

Lester, Julius. *The Blues Singers: Ten Who Rocked the World*. Illustrated by Lisa Cohen. New York: Jump at the Sun/Hyperion Books for Children, 2001.

Medearis, Angela Shelf. *Princess of the Press: The Story of Ida B. Wells-Barnett*. New York: Lodestar Books, 1997.

O'Connor, Barbara. *Katherine Dunham: Pioneer of Black Dance*. Minneapolis: Carolrhoda Books, 1999.

Patterson, Lillie. *A. Phillip Randolph: A Messenger to the Masses*. Broomall, Penn.: Chelsea House Juniors, 1991.

Pinkney, Andrea Davis. *Duke Ellington: The Prince of the Piano and His Orchestra*. Illustrated by J. Brian Pinkney. New York: Hyperion Books for Children, 1998.

Schroeder, Alan. *Booker T. Washington*. Broomall, Penn.: Chelsea House, 1992.

Thomas, Velma Maia. *Freedom's Children: The Passage from Emancipation into the Twentieth Century*. New York: Crown, 2000.

WEBSITES

American Memory from the Library of Congress
http://memory.loc.gov/ammem/ndlpedu/features/timeline/civilwar/civilwar.html

CHICO: Cultural Heritage Initiative for Community Outreach http://www.si.umich.edu/CHICO/Harlem/

Duke University
http://www.duke.edu/~ldbaker/classes/AAIH/caaih/ibwells/ibwbkgrd.html

Tuskegee Airmen Inc.
http://tuskegeeairmen.org/

www.watson.org
http://www.watson.org/~lisa/blackhistory/early-civilrights/

INDEX

abolition of slavery, 11, 58
accommodation policy, 34–35, 37, 38
"Ain't I Glad I've Got Out the Wilderness," 56
Air Force, 47
apprenticeship laws, 8

baseball, 49–51, 58
Bechet, Sidney, 41
Black Codes, 14, 20
black elected officials, 18–19
black soldiers, 6, 46–47, 58
blues, 40, 41
boll weevil, 40
Brooklyn Dodgers, 49–51
Brown, Linda, 54
Brown v. Board of Education of Topeka, Kansas, 54–56, 58

Carter, Robert, 52
children, 8, 30, 31, 38, 52–53, 55
churches, 30
citizenship, 14, 58
civil rights laws, 14, 58
Civil War, 6, 11, 58
Clark, Kenneth, 52–53
Clifton, Lucille, 5
color line, 38, 49
Confederacy, 6, 14
Constitution, 11, 14, 17, 18, 24, 52, 58
convict leasing, 26–27
Cotton Club, 44
cotton crops, 40
Crisis, The, 38
Cullen, Countee, 25

Davis, Benjamin O., Jr., 47
defense industries, 40, 46, 58
desegregation, 46, 47, 56–57, 58
discrimination, 14, 22, 46, 47, 49, 58
Douglass, Frederick, 6, 30, 58
Du Bois, W. E. B., 38
Dunbar, Paul Laurence, 37
Dunham, Katherine, 43

education. See schools
Emancipation Proclamation, 6, 8, 58
equal protection, 24
equal rights, 38, 56, 58
Exodusters, 20–21, 58

Fifteenth Amendment, 18, 58
Fourteenth Amendment, 14, 17, 24, 52, 58

"Free at Last," 12
Freedmen's Bureau, 8, 13, 58
Furbush, W. Hines, 18, 19

Gaines, Matthew, 18, 19
Garvey, Marcus, 43
grandfather clauses, 18, 38, 58

Harlem Renaissance, 43–44, 58
Hope, John, 38
Houston, Charles, 56
Hughes, Langston, 44–45
Hurston, Zora Neale, 43

"If you don't believe I'm sinking," 41
"Incident," 25
indentured servants, 8
"I, Too, Sing America," 45

jazz, 40, 41, 43
"John Henry," 31
Johnson, J. Rosamond, 38
Johnson, James P., 43
Johnson, James Weldon, 38

Kansas, 20–21, 58
Kemper, Jane, 8
kidnappings, 8
Ku Klux Klan, 14–17, 18

Langston, John Mercer, 18, 19
Lawrence, Jacob, 43
Lewis, John Solomon, 20–21
"Lift Ev'ry Voice and Sing," 38–39, 43
"Lifting as We Climb" motto, 30
Lincoln, Abraham, 6, 38
"listen children," 5
Lynch, John R., 18, 19
lynchings, 28–29, 38

Marshall, Thurgood, 52–57
Mays, Benjamin, 30
music, 12, 31, 39, 40–41, 43

National Association for the Advancement of Colored People (NAACP), 38, 52, 58
National Association of Colored Women, 30
Negro in Our History, The, 43
Negro National Anthem, 38
Niagara Movement, 38
northern migration, 40, 43

Pinchback, P. B. S., 18, 19
Plessy, Homer, 24

Plessy v. Ferguson, 24, 52, 58
poll tax, 18, 58
Postle, Harriet, 14–17

railroads, 22–24
Randolph, A. Philip, 46, 47
Rickey, Branch, 49
Robinson, Jackie, 48–51, 58
Rock, John S., 18, 19
Roosevelt, Franklin D., 46, 58

Savage, Augusta, 43
Schomburg, Arthur, 43
schools, 13, 30, 32, 52–57, 58
segregation, 22–24, 38, 44, 46, 47, 52–57, 58
"separate but equal" law, 22, 24, 52, 56, 58
sharecropping, 20, 26, 40
"Shuffle Along" (musical), 43
songs, 12, 31, 38–39, 40, 41, 56
Souls of Black Folk, The, 38
Spicer, Laura, 13
stock market crash, 46
suffrage. See voting rights
Supreme Court, 8, 24, 38, 52, 54–56, 58

Thirteenth Amendment, 11, 58
Townsend, William, 8
Trotter, Monroe, 38
Truman, Harry S., 47, 58
Truth, Sojourner, 30
Tubman, Harriet, 30
Tuskegee Airmen, 47
Tuskegee Institute, 32

"uplift" philosophy, 32, 34

voting rights, 18, 58

Waller, Fats, 43
Warren, Earl, 56
Washington, Booker T., 11, 32–38, 58
Wells, Ida B., 22–24, 28, 38, 58
"We Wear the Mask," 37
white violence, 14–17, 18, 28–29, 37
women's associations, 30
Woodson, Carter G., 43
work songs, 40
World War I, 40, 44, 58
World War II, 46–47

For Eli Zaretsky.
Through the years, your encouragement
and honest, critical assessments have helped me bring children
the most up-to-date historical research in a dynamic fashion.
D. R.

Thank you, God.
Dedicated to my father, Jackie V. Evans,
and to all of those who have worked hard for freedom
so we could all fulfill our dreams.
S. W. E.

The author extends special thanks to Gregg Hammerquist for his technical expertise and generosity.

Text copyright © 2004 by Doreen Rappaport
Illustrations copyright © 2004 by Shane W. Evans

First edition 2004

Library of Congress Cataloging-in-Publication Data
Rappaport, Doreen.
Free at last! : stories and songs of Emancipation / Doreen Rappaport ; illustrated by Shane W. Evans. — 1st ed.
p. cm.
Summary: Describes the experiences of African Americans in the South, from Emancipation in 1863
to the 1954 Supreme Court decision that declared school segregation illegal.
ISBN 0-7636-1440-8
1. African Americans — History — 1863-1877 — Miscellanea — Juvenile literature. 2. African Americans — History — 1877-1964 —
Miscellanea — Juvenile literature. 3. African Americans — Civil rights — History — Miscellanea — Juvenile literature.
4. Southern states — Race relations — Miscellanea — Juvenile literature. [1. African Americans — History — 1863-1877.
2. African Americans — History — 1877-1964. 3. African Americans — Civil rights.] I. Evans, Shane, ill. II. Title.
E185.2.R27 2004
973'.0496073 — dc21   2003043853

2 4 6 8 10 9 7 5 3 1

Printed in Italy

This book was typeset in Integrity.
The illustrations were done in oil.

Candlewick Press
2067 Massachusetts Avenue
Cambridge, Massachusetts 02140

visit us at www.candlewick.com